T4-AEG-549

FOUNDATIONS OF OUR NATION

THE AMERICAN REVOLUTION

by Clara MacCarald

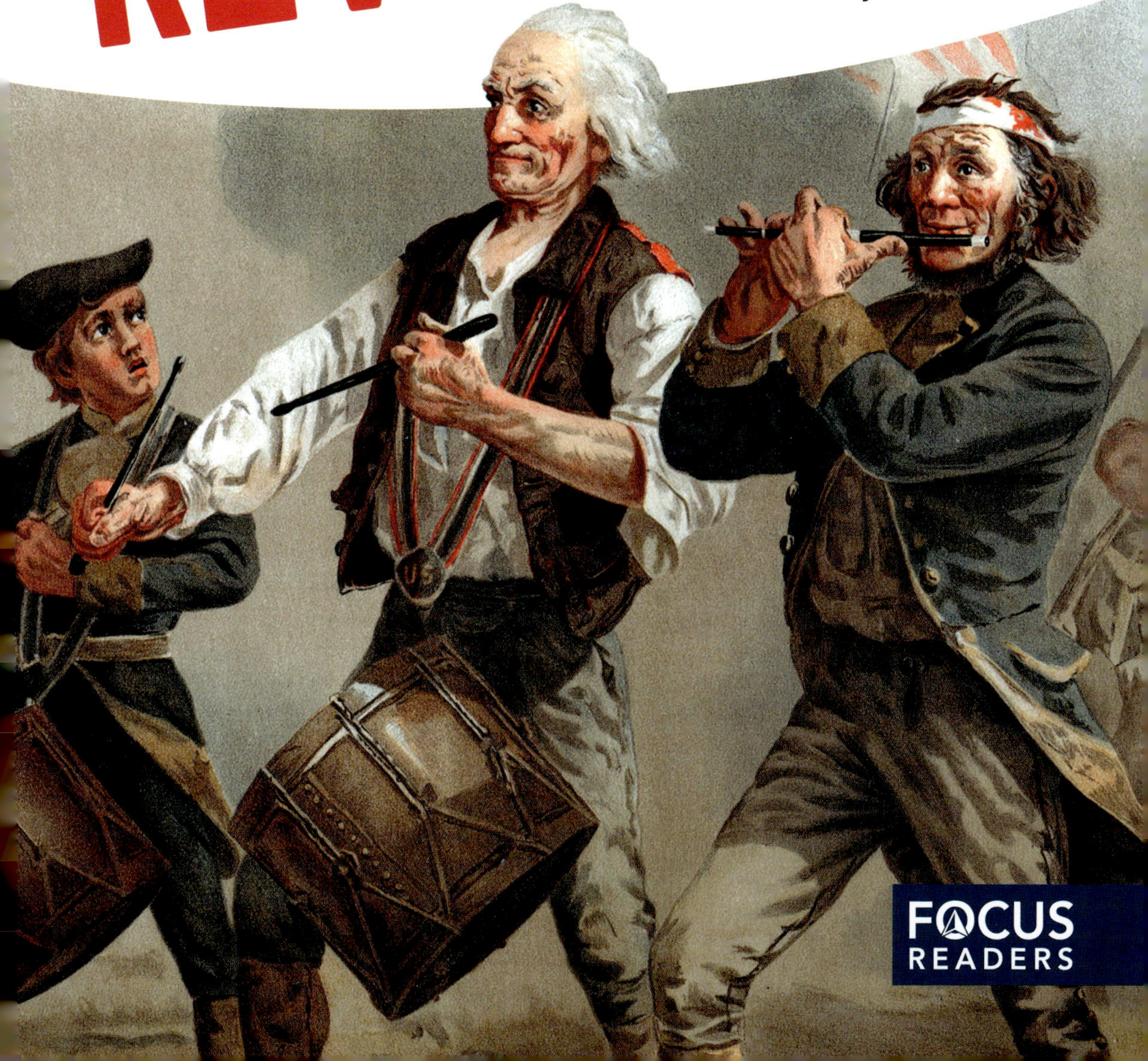

FOCUS READERS

www.focusreaders.com

Copyright © 2018 by Focus Readers, Lake Elmo, MN 55042. All rights reserved. No part of this book may be reproduced or utilized in any form or by any means without written permission from the publisher.

Focus Readers is distributed by North Star Editions: sales@northstareditions.com | 888-417-0195

Produced for Focus Readers by Red Line Editorial.

Content Consultant: Dr. Gideon Mailer, Associate Professor of History, University of Minnesota Duluth

Photographs ©: Everett Historical/Shutterstock Images, cover, 1; North Wind Picture Archives, 4–5, 7, 10–11, 13, 17, 20–21, 23, 26–27, 29; Red Line Editorial, 9, 19; Alexander Hay Ritchie/Library of Congress, 14–15; Album/Oronoz/Newscom, 25

ISBN
978-1-63517-242-3 (hardcover)
978-1-63517-307-9 (paperback)
978-1-63517-437-3 (ebook pdf)
978-1-63517-372-7 (hosted ebook)

Library of Congress Control Number: 2017935936

Printed in the United States of America
Mankato, MN
June, 2017

ABOUT THE AUTHOR

Clara MacCarald is a freelance writer with a master's degree in biology. She lives with her family in an off-grid house nestled in the forests of central New York. When not parenting her daughter, she spends her time writing nonfiction books for kids.

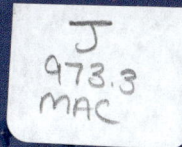

TABLE OF CONTENTS

CHAPTER 1
The Seeds of Revolution 5

CHAPTER 2
Struggle for Power 11

CHAPTER 3
Armed Revolution 15

CHAPTER 4
Making Peace 21

VOICES FROM THE PAST
Chickasaws React 24

CHAPTER 5
A New Nation Rises 27

Focus on the American Revolution • 30
Glossary • 31
To Learn More • 32
Index • 32

CHAPTER 1

THE SEEDS OF REVOLUTION

In 1763, the Seven Years' War came to an end. The war had involved many nations. Great Britain and its **allies** were victorious. They defeated France, Spain, and several other countries. But fighting the war had been very expensive. Leaders in Great Britain decided the American colonists should help pay the costs.

British soldiers launch an attack on the French during the Seven Years' War.

In 1765, the British Parliament passed the Stamp Act. This act forced colonists to pay taxes on certain goods. It required them to buy special stamped papers. The papers showed that the taxes had been paid.

Many colonists believed Parliament did not have the right to tax them. After all, the colonists did not have **representatives** in Parliament. To make their anger known, some colonists refused to buy British goods. The protests spread, and Parliament ended the Stamp Act in 1766. However, Great Britain's leaders still believed in their power over the colonies.

Colonists in New York City burn stamps to protest the Stamp Act.

Parliament soon created more taxes. To keep the peace, Great Britain sent soldiers to the colonies. But on March 5, 1770, crowds of angry colonists roamed the streets of Boston, Massachusetts.

7

They were armed with clubs and swords. A mob started attacking some of the soldiers with snowballs and ice. The soldiers opened fire, killing five colonists. The colonists were outraged. They called this event the Boston Massacre.

Tempers continued to run high in the following years. The colonists did not like Great Britain's tax on tea, which was a popular drink. On the night of December 16, 1773, dozens of colonists swarmed onto three ships in Boston Harbor. The ships carried hundreds of tea chests. The tea was very valuable. But the colonists smashed the chests and tossed the tea into the water. A crowd cheered them on.

Opposition to the British government was growing.

NORTH AMERICA AFTER THE SEVEN YEARS' WAR

After winning the Seven Years' War, Great Britain gained most of eastern North America. A 1763 law tried to stop colonists from moving west of the Appalachian Mountains. This territory was home to many American Indian nations.

CHAPTER 2

STRUGGLE FOR POWER

Leaders in Great Britain knew they had to respond to the colonists' actions. So, Parliament passed a series of laws. One law shut down Boston Harbor. Another took power away from the Massachusetts colony. Colonists disliked these laws. They referred to them as the Intolerable Acts.

British soldiers arrive in Boston after the colonists' protest.

The colonists had to figure out how to respond. They sent representatives to a meeting. It was known as the Continental Congress. The representatives knew Great Britain would not end the Intolerable Acts without pressure. So, they decided the colonies would **boycott** British goods. This action would harm the British economy.

	Each colony formed groups to **enforce** the boycott. These groups began taking control of local **militias**. The militias gathered many weapons. They hid the weapons from British soldiers. Then, in April 1775, colonists discovered a secret plan. British troops were planning to

British troops fight with a colonial militia in Lexington, setting off the American Revolutionary War.

leave Boston soon. They were going to destroy a militia's stash of weapons in the nearby town of Concord. Halfway to Concord, the British fought with colonial militia forces in the town of Lexington. When the British reached Concord, they found armed colonists. The militia chased the British back to Boston. The American **Revolutionary** War had begun.

CHAPTER 3

ARMED REVOLUTION

News of the battles spread through the colonies. The British remained in Boston. Meanwhile, the Continental Congress met again in 1775. This time they had a war to manage. They created the Continental Army and chose George Washington to lead it.

Washington meets with his generals during the American Revolutionary War.

The colonists were at war. However, they still had not agreed on what they were fighting for. Did they want better laws under British rule? Or did they want **independence**? Finally, on July 4, 1776, the Continental Congress approved the Declaration of Independence. This document said the United States was a new nation.

The British would not give up their colonies without a fight. In the fall of 1776, they defeated Washington's army in New York City. But on December 26, the Continental Army sneaked into Trenton, New Jersey. They captured hundreds of soldiers. Americans also won a battle in

Washington leads his troops at the Battle of Princeton.

Princeton, New Jersey. These two events lifted the Americans' spirits.

A separate British army fought its way south through New York state. A large force of Americans surrounded them at Saratoga, New York. The British surrendered in October 1777.

This victory showed other countries that the Americans had a chance of winning the war. The French soon agreed to side with the Americans. Other countries later helped the Americans as well.

Not all colonists were **patriots** who fought for independence. Some were **loyalists** who supported the British.

Black people joined both sides. Many gained freedom from slavery by serving in the army. American Indians fought on both sides, too.

In early 1778, a German officer taught the Americans new fighting skills. This helped them face the British in the summer. The French provided many supplies. In 1781, the Americans and French cornered a large part of the British army in Yorktown, Virginia. The British surrendered on October 19. The last major battle of the war was over.

TIMELINE OF MAJOR BATTLES

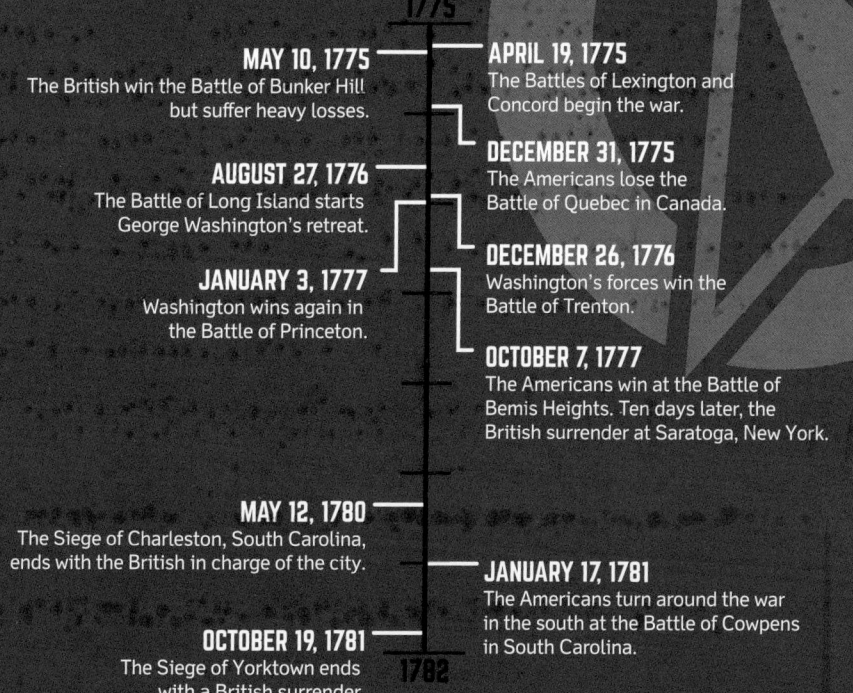

1775

MAY 10, 1775
The British win the Battle of Bunker Hill but suffer heavy losses.

APRIL 19, 1775
The Battles of Lexington and Concord begin the war.

DECEMBER 31, 1775
The Americans lose the Battle of Quebec in Canada.

AUGUST 27, 1776
The Battle of Long Island starts George Washington's retreat.

DECEMBER 26, 1776
Washington's forces win the Battle of Trenton.

JANUARY 3, 1777
Washington wins again in the Battle of Princeton.

OCTOBER 7, 1777
The Americans win at the Battle of Bemis Heights. Ten days later, the British surrender at Saratoga, New York.

MAY 12, 1780
The Siege of Charleston, South Carolina, ends with the British in charge of the city.

JANUARY 17, 1781
The Americans turn around the war in the south at the Battle of Cowpens in South Carolina.

OCTOBER 19, 1781
The Siege of Yorktown ends with a British surrender.

1782

CHAPTER 4

MAKING PEACE

Most of the fighting had ended, but the war was not officially over. Word of the British surrender traveled across the ocean. The news rocked the British government. In March 1782, Great Britain decided to make peace. The countries started working on a treaty.

British soldiers surrender to American forces in Yorktown, Virginia.

Meanwhile, the American states were trying to figure out how to pay their soldiers. The states did not like the idea of creating taxes. But without taxes, soldiers could not be paid. By 1783, the Continental Army was becoming restless. Some soldiers wanted to take control of the government. But Washington delivered a speech to his army. He convinced them to wait for payment.

     The countries signed the peace treaty on September 3, 1783. It was known as the Treaty of Paris. Great Britain recognized the United States as an independent nation. The United States gained the land between the Atlantic

Washington and his army enter New York City after winning the war.

coast and the Mississippi River. Spain took back Florida. It had been a Spanish colony before the Seven Years' War.

The American Indians that allied with Great Britain were no longer protected. These allies included the Senecas and Delawares. Many American settlers took over their land. In time, even tribes that fought with the Americans lost their land to settlers.

23

VOICES FROM THE PAST

CHICKASAWS REACT

The Chickasaw nation lived near Georgia and Florida. During the war, they had been allies of Great Britain. In July 1783, they sent a letter to the American government. "The King of England called away his warriors," they wrote. "He told us to take your people by the hand as friends and brothers."

But the Chickasaws were unhappy. Americans settlers "want part of our land," they wrote. "And we expect our neighbors . . . will in a little time . . . take part of it from us."

The Chickasaws hoped to keep their land by becoming American allies. "Our hearts are always with our brothers the Americans," they said. But in the 1830s, the US government forced the

American Indians make the difficult journey to Oklahoma. Their forced relocation is known as the Trail of Tears.

Chickasaws to leave their homeland. Today most Chickasaws live in Oklahoma.

CHAPTER 5

A NEW NATION RISES

In November 1783, British soldiers marched to the New York City harbor. They set sail. They were the last part of the British army to leave. Washington and his troops paraded into town. The new nation had defeated one of the greatest military powers in the world.

The last British troops leave the United States after losing the war.

The United States was still recovering from the war. Tens of thousands had died. Money was scarce. But Americans felt a new sense of freedom. They were free from rule from afar. They had created a **republic**. Representatives were elected by American citizens.

But not everyone rejoiced. Tens of thousands of loyalists left the United States. They moved to other parts of the British Empire. Of those who stayed, not all were treated equally. Women did not have the same rights as men. Black people were forced into slavery. These problems were not addressed for many years.

Slavery was legal in parts of the United States until 1865.

After the war, the US government struggled to raise money. It also had problems dealing with other nations. Some leaders decided the United States needed a stronger government. In 1787, representatives from the states held a meeting. They wrote the US Constitution. The document they created is still central to the US government today.

FOCUS ON THE AMERICAN REVOLUTION

Write your answers on a separate piece of paper.

1. Write a letter to a friend describing what you learned about the causes of the American Revolution.

2. Do you think the colonists were right to protest the Stamp Act? Why or why not?

3. What event led to Parliament passing the Intolerable Acts?
    - **A.** The Boston Massacre
    - **B.** The Boston Tea Party
    - **C.** The Battle of Lexington

4. What might have happened if Washington had not calmed the Continental Army in 1783?
    - **A.** The army may have taken over the US government.
    - **B.** The army may have attacked Great Britain.
    - **C.** The army may have attacked Canada.

Answer key on page 32.

GLOSSARY

allies
Nations or people that are on the same side during a war.

boycott
To refuse to buy certain goods as a form of protest.

enforce
To make sure people follow a rule.

independence
The ability to make decisions without being controlled by another government.

loyalists
Colonists who supported Great Britain.

militias
Military forces formed by ordinary people trained to fight.

patriots
Colonists who supported independence.

representatives
People who speak on behalf of a larger group.

republic
A form of government in which power is held by people and their elected representatives.

revolutionary
Having to do with a complete change in government.

TO LEARN MORE

BOOKS

Murphy, Jim. *The Crossing: How George Washington Saved the American Revolution*. New York: Scholastic, 2010.

Murray, Stuart. *American Revolution*. New York: DK, 2015.

Woelfle, Gretchen. *Answering the Cry for Freedom: Stories of African Americans and the American Revolution*. Honesdale, PA: Calkins Creek, 2016.

NOTE TO EDUCATORS

Visit www.focusreaders.com to find lesson plans, activities, links, and other resources related to this title.

INDEX

American Indians, 18, 23–25

Boston Massacre, 8

Chickasaws, 24–25
Concord, Massachusetts, 13
Constitution, 29
Continental Army, 15–16, 22
Continental Congress, 12, 15–16

Declaration of Independence, 16
Delawares, 23

France, 5, 18–19

Intolerable Acts, 11–12

Lexington, Massachusetts, 13

New York City, 16, 27

Princeton, New Jersey, 17

Saratoga, New York, 17
Senecas, 23
Seven Years' War, 5, 23
Spain, 5, 23
Stamp Act, 6

Treaty of Paris, 22
Trenton, New Jersey, 16

Washington, George, 15–16, 22, 27

Yorktown, Virginia, 19

Answer Key: 1. Answers will vary; 2. Answers will vary; 3. B; 4. A